GATHER ENOUGH FIREFLIES

―

To Bart,
and to
Cole

Gather Enough Fireflies

by Suzi Tucker

Julius Books

JULIUS BOOKS
P.O. Box 458
Redding Ridge, CT 06876

Copyright © 2014 by SUZI TUCKER

All rights reserved.
No part of this book may be
reproduced by any process
whatsoever without the written
permission of the copyright owner.

ISBN-10: 0990773302
ISBN-13: 978-0-9907733-0-6

Cover design and interior design:
COLE TUCKER-WALTON

Set in Baskerville.

suzitucker.com
facebook.com/guidedlearning

Gather Enough Fireflies is a series of contributions centered on essential threads that connect us, and sometimes separate us – one from another, one from the present, self from self.

Part One: 1

Part Two: 103

A Little Background: 177

A Guide to the Entries: 181

Part One

2

GATHER ENOUGH FIREFLIES

Brevities 1

In one of my first personal encounters with Bert Hellinger, I mentioned that my brother had been institutionalized before I was born and that I only found out about him when I was in my early teens. I lived with my mom, and saw my dad on some weekends and holidays. I don't really remember how she told me about my brother, but I think he was ill and she had to make some sort of decision with regard to treatment. I had a brother all along, have one still. Wow. Her guilt, shame, loneliness – I cannot really imagine. At any rate, it was a dramatic moment, but truthfully it had no real meaning to me. I can say that now. He was an abstraction and this revelation was drama, a bit of family theater. At least, I think that's how I understood the whole thing.

So, when I mentioned my brother to Bert all those years later, it still may have been a part of the script I was sharing. After all, Bert taught something called Family Constellations. I may have thought, Hey, I have an unusual family too, I belong here, I am a part. I wasn't so confident in my intelligence or other gifts, but I had this ace in the hole: a forgotten brother. Bert's response was a rather undramatic sentence: Now, I understand why you always sit in the back. I will work with you this afternoon.

A Family Constellation takes place in a group. It is a dimensional exploration of a particular familial field. As participants step in to represent various family members, or sometimes emotional entities, the field rises up and unfolds without direction or intervention. As the image opens, with representatives navigating the relational space, guided by internal resonance with each other and some greater movement, the person who is working may begin to see, and then feel, or the other way around, where his or her problems sit in a larger context. He or she may also be able to glimpse and then later grow the essential life-force that also resides there. Rather than a targeted therapy, there are the natural possibilities that accompany kinesis: an antidote to the mental/physical/soul-level dis-ease that comes with stagnation.

I do not recall all of the elements of the Constellation that Bert facilitated. The fact that both of my great-grandmothers died in childbirth was context, loss and fear and grief and a sense of not-enoughness seeping in through the layers of the generations. The sense memory I have though – from the constellation, which must have recalled a sense memory from a wholly other time zone – was my brother by my side. My older brother standing by my side, filling up my side, with warmth, with being, with total agreement. More than a sense memory it was a sensory revelation. My brother, Edwin, was transformed from the poor, retarded boy, frozen in time, only recalled in order to remember to forget, into a man, my older brother, who protected his baby sister with all his might, and who continues to stand beside me, exactly as he can, neither bending to my childish wishes for him to be other than he is nor collapsing under my guilt or anyone else's. Of course, it's a

PART ONE

misnomer to call this his transformation – it was and is mine. I freed him from the narrowness of my image, and in so doing allowed something essential to shift in my relationship to him, to my mother and father, to myself, to my family field.

Sentences to live by: Thank you, Edwin, for being my older brother. We live in very different ways. We have different voices, touch different people. I will try to do something with the gifts I have been given. Perhaps you will know that I feel you beside me always now, and it is good. And I speak your name in public often. Edwin Friedman.

Constellations bring wide, deep images to the fore. They are not concerned with the stories we tell or the interpretations we have made. We know those. The wider field isn't much aware of the details. Defenses we developed very young, around which we then built philosophies to protect them. In a Constellation, people step into a collaborative perceptual grid where energy, information, sometimes breathtaking (or giving) mysteries are exchanged and/or navigated until the field comes to a place of serenity with everyone and everything included.

PART ONE

So, as my brother moved from being the excluded one, unwittingly caught up in others' blindness and loss, to being seen and acknowledged, appreciated and loved, something settled in the field. Again, perhaps this is a misnomer. It was I who settled – at least, that is my window into the prism. Stepping out of loyalty to the little self of my mother, the part of her that felt too small to stand behind both of her children, I was able to embrace him and to embrace her fully. In that embrace, I stopped taking care of her in a way, and began receiving from her.

Sentences to live by: You gave me life, and I carry your gifts forward. In breaking free from connecting with you solely through pain, those gifts can be used in new ways. When loyalty becomes love, judgment becomes gratitude, and gratitude fuels life. Thank you, Evelyn May Tucker.

Another ripple. It never occurred to me that taking my father back into my heart would in any way be useful or appropriate. For most of my life, righteousness seemed to satisfy me – he was this, he was that, he wasn't there for me, screw him. Over time, though, new images began to emerge when he came to mind. It was a natural movement, effortless. I might describe it as having more space in my body/mind/heart to receive updates to my way of seeing and understanding my own inner geography. He was a fashion illustrator, charming, fearful, loving, handsome, athletic, Hungarian, secretive, a gambler, meticulous, light, so many things, human. And there are others, feelings I can't quite articulate, interests that grab hold, skills and qualities that come to me as gifts I cannot quite trace.

Sentences to live by: You gave me life, and I carry your gifts forward. In breaking free of my little girl's anger and longing, I see you with me when I look in the mirror. You are my only father, and I get to know you now through me. I allow a new relationship to form in my body, with you and Mom showing me the way, no longer split by the old stories. When anger is understood as longing, longing is met with love; love includes gratitude, gratitude fuels life. My father: Edwin Friedman.

PART ONE

Brevities 2

When people are in intimate relationship with their problems, there is little room for moving beyond those problems. The tension of this dyadic relationship fills up the heart space, the head space, the lung space. And a protective shell forms around the relationship, as we hide the problem, like a lover we are embarrassed by, from the world. When the problem is the thing we know best, whether we run like hell from it, or, despite our best efforts, are consumed by it, the problem is the main marker, it is the North Star. Everything else exists in relation to it. The problem is the guide. I will not, I will not; oh no, I am, I am. Again.

In general, our current problems have always been our problems. From way back, we had an awareness of certain areas of dysfunction or stuckness. Over time, there have likely been many variations on the theme, but basically, the problems we have now are in line with the problems we had long ago. The word "problem" is an abbreviation for the way we receive the world.

Like a chronic dieter, we have tried all kinds of strategies and approaches to manage our problem, but somehow we again find ourselves snapping back to old behaviors and feelings – and now with a little more regret, shame, and disappointment heaped on. Like the dieter who gains back the weight and even a little more, we are again and again confronted by the fact that something always proves stronger than our best intentions, than our desires.

Often our problem (or problems) is everything to us. We hate it, yes, want to change it, yes, but would we know ourselves without it? Since the problem usually has been with us a very long time, a reliable companion, even if it has worn different disguises at different times, perhaps we would be disoriented without our problem by our side. It is a strange thought.

Stranger still, what if the problem rather than being primarily an obstacle is more like an anchor, something that keeps us connected with important people from our past, our mother and/or father, for instance, or others in the family?

We usually recognize this on one level. "My mother was depressed too." "I think I am angry just like my father was." "Oh, everyone in my family is completely disconnected. It's crazy." But here we think in terms of a pattern. So we think we may be stuck in a cycle of repetition, something we cannot escape, just as our mother couldn't or our father couldn't or our entire family couldn't. I am thinking about this in another way.

Why would we be powerless to interrupt a pattern we see, and deem destructive? We see others caught in it, are angry (or sad or disappointed) about them, so, what holds us in the same place?

What if doing better than they did (or do) feels unbearable on some level? What if, in the end, not abandoning Mom to sadness or

Dad to addiction feels more real, more important, than pursuing our own hopes and dreams? What if more than simply being part of a pattern, the continuation of a certain behavior is actually an expression of fear or love or both?

From this perspective, we see that through the problem, we have taken a position. We will stand with, we will stand guard, we will protect, sacrifice, and hang back from the present and from the future. Staying in the sphere of sadness with Mom or anger with Dad, I express devotion, stronger even than my own desires. It leads to further anger and sadness, of course, but more about that later.

For now, if we begin to toy with the idea of our depression, anger, disconnection, or whatever, as a way to stay with people who were and are essential to our life (even once they are gone), perhaps we can begin to imagine new and better ways to acknowledge those longings. We can look for the key to break free of the redundancy. It is a creative proposition. The original image, the image we are born into, sets this kind of deep belonging into motion. Connection begins where our lives began, with our parents.

Brevities 3

Change is a process, not a place. You have heard it before. What does it mean? It's an important thing to remember, even before settling on meaning. A process implies movement, a series of steps. Process is a moving idea. It is active, building, onward. Pattern, on the other hand, is inactive, a series of sames.

Part One

Brevities 4

We cannot fix the past, our own or others'. But the sense that maybe we can trips us up even as we remember that change is a process. This is a common experience. We turn our attention to what is already past, already gone, and try to "fix" it. Ah but when someone or something is fixed, it also means that he or she or it is stopped, fixed in place, fastened to a moment in time, to an image that we hold. And we too are fixed on that image. Standing with our back to life, engaged in a futile transaction that feeds on itself, standing perfectly still, and yet exhausted, we are fixed on the image: it was bad, I can make it better. Going back to the problem, the fixed image – and its imagined reparation – takes a lot of energy and gives back little. This is an uncreative proposition. If my mother hadn't, If I hadn't, If god hadn't … I will get her to change, I will make up for everything, I will rail against you, demand that you save me, and wait for the sign (no, not that one, another one).

A better image, perhaps, is that nothing is "fixed" once life and love are moving again. Not fixed, new possibility emerges – as life is continually presenting new opportunity – and we can see ourselves in flow, even from the broken what was, into a process of change, into a burgeoning and transformative reciprocity with life as it is coming toward us right in this moment, in the timeless and fleeting now.

Simultaneously, reparation of the past is, on a deeper level, naturally achieved when the future unfolds in a good way. When there is great hardship and strife at one point (or at many points) on a continuum, it is only the good outcome that has enough weight to meet that hardship and strife. A mother who dies in childbirth lives on in her child. The better that child does, the better the mother does. The same is so across circumstances, more or less dramatic. Of course, if we are freed from the obligation to fix the issue, and indeed enjoined to use that freedom in a good way, what happens next? We know what happens when we hold tight to the past, staying in intimate connection with our pain and the pain of others. It may be frustrating, sad, infuriating, but we know what to expect. What happens when we don't?

Part One

Brevities 5

It is clear that we know immediately what our family system needs from us upon birth, what we need to provide in exchange for survival. We accept the assignment, whatever it is, as a matter of life and death. This family, this tribe, this system, this first group – we rely on them for everything. For nine months, she provided everything necessary to live. Our life was at one with hers. She and they gave life; they can take it away. For a time this is absolutely true, a clear and straightforward understanding. Although we live by the sense memory long past the literal truth of it, that sense is founded on an accurate perception, an accurate reception of encoded messages free-floating in the ether of the system: we need, we are sad, we are weak, we are scared, we cannot bear anymore, we have been through so much. And so, our answer must be: I will give, I will be sad too, I will be strong above all else and demand nothing, I will protect you even though I'm scared too, I won't be a nuisance, I won't cause more trouble.

Much later in life and throughout it, we generally are still negotiating and renegotiating both the commitments we made to uphold those early agreements and our desire to break the contracts, weighing one against the other. Most of the time though, the view is the same. We have grown older, but the vantage point is the same. To reject or to merge still feel like the only options. Of course, these are actually the same option; either way, that first understanding, that first signature, is providing the information as to what is possible and okay, and what is not. Will they survive my happiness? Will I survive my own happiness?

GATHER ENOUGH FIREFLIES

Brevities 6

The answer absolutely is time travel. When we were very young, a baby in somebody's arms – maybe our mother, perhaps our father, in some cases others who took care – it was the survival dyad. That was it: deep, total, endless, everything. If there was anger, that was the milk. If there was fear, that was the milk. If there was grief, that was the milk. No relationship was ever so clear, an encapsulated dyad in an otherwise chaotic environment of explosive sound and light, sudden dark, and heat, smooth surface, rough hands, and a thousand other incomprehensible sensations. Attuned to this one dyad was survival, was it.

If we go back in time, which of course we can (we do it all the time in negative ways), we can adjust our lens from zoom to wide angle.

Returning to the original image, the first information, we see ourselves, the baby in someone's arms. But returning now, all these years on, we watch from a distance.

Perhaps close your eyes; read this first and then close your eyes and see if you can bring your original image into view – and then expand it. We notice that the person who holds this child, this us from long ago, actually has others behind him or her. There are several close by, offering their support, many more behind these, and as we lift our head to see further, we can imagine tens, hundreds, thousands, as many as we can hold in our imaginations, watching over the one who holds this baby – us – and we can feel in our present body a small release. The dyad that was can begin to soften into a larger landscape. The care that we once understood was our job to give begins to be taken over by those who can actually provide what is needed. And they can help the one in whose arms we struggle or coo or lie placidly hold us. We can feel that now, in this moment, as past and present merge in a completely new way … not through our "problem" but through love and through gratitude. Somehow we made it.

When, for example, we see our mother, who feels to us endlessly needy, in her own mother's arms, and beyond that all the mothers and fathers, we are released from the duty that we took on in our innocence and fear when we were too young. At the same time, we are freed to receive the best from her, to let that be real inside of us, and to, finally, cause some trouble, because from this vantage point we see that she can take it, by becoming all that we wish to be. In return, at rest in her mother's arms and beyond that in the arms of all who came before, we can see a smile come to her face. In our blossoming, she can feel that she has done well. The dynamics we were born into, all of the survival knowledge we knew for certain long ago, can become blurred, soft, more spacious now.

This is an image. We live from images. We take actions, form relationships, make choices, all based on images. The felt image of the too-small child faced with endless, all-consuming tasks can begin to be transformed. The baby-child-adolescent-young-adult has done the job as it was understood, done it well. It can be enough now. The adult who returns once more to look again, the time traveler, who returns to gather more than the original knowledge, can indeed allow the wider picture of the past to soon be reflected in the wider picture of a wholly new present. The expanding image becomes an expanding range of actions, relationships, choices.

GATHER ENOUGH FIREFLIES

Brevities 7

The replication of past situations in present circumstances is not only an exercise in futility as far as altering what was, it also leeches the life-force from the individual engaged in it. Replication here may mean literally playing out dynamics over and over again in different situations, or it may mean that the subconscious is captivated by the past and thus at odds, or out of sync, with the conscious mind and what we desire in the present. There is energy-sapping discontinuity between the draw to the past (the problem) and our attempts to reenter the present-into-future. Eventually, the "juice" seems to run dangerously low. Maybe we feel depleted, hopeless, sick, old, uncaring, empty, disconnected, judgmental, angry, confused. These are signals that life-force, the instinct of all of life to move forward, is pooling inside of us with no outlet and that it is threatening to drown us.

When operating from the trance of the past it is impossible to be fully present. By trance, I mean the subconscious drift toward old places outside of current reality. Dealing with present things from this distance tends to be confusing: what am I looking at? Exhausting: why am I not enough? Disconnecting: I don't understand what is going on. Judgment-inducing: I give up, and project onto you all that I hate about me because it feels momentarily consoling. And the juice level goes down a bit more.

Life-force is that thing that we draw from to rise each day, that buoys us through challenge, and that we are most acutely aware of in love. Everyone before us had it. They each and all allowed it to flow through them and then from them, whether in great or small degrees, into the future, to wash over, and to touch in a thousand unexpected ways. For each and all, the momentum, the life-force, the juice, had no mind, no rationale, no strategy (though the individuals who carried it undoubtedly thought they had). Through war and hunger and many ends-of-world, life-force insisted on coming through. Thus to be out of accord with it, to attempt to stay still as life rushes forward, rushes past, is a high-stakes stance for an individual.

For life, of course, it doesn't really matter. Our resistance means little in the big scheme of things, though it means a lot to us and to those who are close, especially our children. Life doesn't care whether or not we participate, whether or not we find meaning. Life is enriched by our contribution but it is not diminished by our lack of one. That's a humbling thought.

Being in present time allows access to life-force – and outlet. We release ourselves from the old and stale stories into the ongoing flow of life-force. There, we can ride the energy of forward movement. We can be alert for obstacles and opportunities, seeing people and things for what they are, not as reflections or projections of stagnant images. When we are fully present to the present, we can handle things lightly as they come: even heavy experience is lighter when we are present to it. Negotiating the present from elsewhere is like reaching for something on the tippy-top shelf without a ladder. We cannot quite see what's up there; the reaching up is fatiguing; our grip is tenuous; our balance is threatened; we are not at ease and we are not prepared, whether the top shelf turns out to hold something nutritious and refreshing or something debilitating, even destructive.

Brevities 8

Why is it that we ask advice from others, and then so rarely follow the advice? Even when the advisor is wise, and we believe it, what she or he has to tell us slips right out of reach, out of meaning. We listen, what is said makes sense, is even deemed right in the moment of listening. But advice, good or not, needs to feel aligned with our inner geography if it's going to be used to positive effect. If our stance is shut down to life-force (as described above), then the advice we receive, even if we attempt to apply it, will have little chance of success. Take the job, marry the man, move to where you are not, stand up, sit down, forgive, release, build up, break down … none of the external modifications has a chance against a narrow inner landscape. Happiness is an aspect of language; being happy is a matter of fluency. Advice – perspectives on stuff from outside the Self – cannot be applied, really, or judged appropriately, without an inner stance that supports the basic flow of life.

When someone asks me for advice, I might wonder how she is looking at the given topic. Where is she standing? If the decision is supposed to shift life in any meaningful way, it needs to be attuned to an already established sense of shift and meaning.

When we place something lively into a stagnant pond, there is little chance that it will thrive.

On the other hand, once we have returned to our original images and allowed the lens to widen to gather in more support, more context, more triumph, we allow the momentum of life to take over. Once life-force is a presumption, the great and simple gift from those who came before, replenishing that life-force becomes a more natural correspondence. And so the choices we make can be in accord with a movement toward more life, and we can allow ourselves really to know when the "yes" or "no" to

Part One

something or someone adds or takes away from that movement.

Meaningful projects and goals are important – markers and milestones – but at the same time, it is essential to realize that everything isn't contingent upon them working out in a certain way, according to a plan made at the beginning. The plan must shift along the way, be in tune with the shifting rhythms and waves of life, while at the same time upholding the original vision.

When I say "yes" to the job, for instance, because I see it as being in accord with the movement toward more life (which includes such mundane and unromantic aspects as being able to pay my rent), then I will enter the situation in a good way. I am open to accomplishment, to interest, to gratitude. I can be easy with the goodness and the challenge, celebrate what works, and allow what doesn't to be at a low ebb. This is the face I show to the environment – grateful and easy, hopeful, but not starving.

And if the job turns out to be wrong for me, I can allow myself to know that too, allow it to be simple knowledge, important, but not devastating. The job is not as I thought; it is not in accord with what for me is "toward more." The fit is off, or it is downright horrible. Either way, I have an inner sense – resonant with the generations – of moving toward more, making something of the gift I have been given, and my knowledge can be acted upon in a good way, in accord with a stance already in place. When the past is "triggered" by the present situation, clarity, timing, and positive response go out the window. In accord with the present, I see with clarity that my "yes" was merely misplaced, or perfectly placed but impermanent, and I can begin to take steps to find the next "yes." I can act efficaciously but not precipitously. Not the child, either pushing Mother away entirely or being too terrified to say what she needs, but rather the adult, who, having returned to receive more from the more, can be at greater ease with the continuous unfolding of life.

PART ONE

Brevities 9

Living in the confusion between past and present, everyday decisions often feel overwhelming. We think we are abnormal in being overwhelmed by the common questions, which adds to the discontinuity between what we desire and what we feel capable of. But when we continue to open the landscape, we often see that the systemic dynamics that affect us were initiated further back than our parents.

When we think about what prevents us from quitting or following through or initiating or anything else that might logically make life better, sometimes a feeling in our body is what we can really locate – the thoughts in our head are already second-hand – a feeling of breathlessness or trembling or paralysis ignite those second-hand ideas. What is that feeling? What is on the other side of it? Perhaps it's something really far-fetched like, "I'll disappear," or "I'll be killed," or "I just cannot bear being alone."

Perhaps take a moment, allow the problem or decision to enter your mind. I cannot stand my job. My marriage is horrible. I want to stop drinking. I am so insecure. Whatever it is named, let it in. Then feel the words in your body. What comes up? How would you describe the feeling in your body to someone else? I cannot breathe. My head hurts. Everything goes blank. It clusters behind my eyes and presses against my temples.

Again, a little time travel. These dramatic feelings around mundane problems make us feel crazy, or at least peculiar. The drama queen, the crybaby, the raging bitch, the little mouse, the ... mean names we call ourselves, may be called by others. But when we go back a generation or two or three, we may find exactly where the feelings make absolute sense, are right-sized responses as opposed to crazy reactions.

Let's imagine: Where in your history was the price of speaking up too high, even death? Where was a complaint or condition received without compassion? Where did success – intelligence, talent, a knack for something – endanger life? Where are there perpetrators who could not face their own guilt or despair? Where are there victims who could not face their own anger or sense of defeat? Where did some benefit on the backs of others? Where did some abandon others in order to go on?

For whom do we atone? Fight? Punish the men? The women? Put aside our dreams?

PART ONE

Destroy our reality? Belittle possibility? Stay behind?

What has not ended in our hearts, in our deep and visceral life, the life that teems with hidden energy, not sanctioned or even seen by our awareness?

The events to which we connect concern life and death, actions that caused the family system to lose its traction, either completely or momentarily, and then head in another direction. War, for example, changes the course of thousands of systems – victims and perpetrators – so that new survival vocabularies evolve, and with them new depths of grief, anger, distrust. Then too the boy who loses his father when he is three years old: his course is inexorably shifted. In either case, the next generations will be navigating life and death even as they are moving across the simpler plain of daily living.

The original belonging – to our family of origin – is where we receive the information that has the greatest impact of any other information we ever receive. We have no ability to resist those messages. Some of the messages have been carried through generations, landing in us inadvertently. Events of the past can fragment the family for decades to come, leaving people to clamor for balance, visibility, justice, peace, or anger. The events that happened so long ago, even beyond our memory, can affect us powerfully. Free-floating anxiety or grief or terror may travel down to us, and we take it on without deliberation, without the wherewithal or time to deliberate. Now, the feelings are without context, or they appear to be inconsistent with context, with the one that is visible. And yet, to our great frustration or worse, our hearts are captured and we seem bound and gagged when it comes to the present.

Uncovering an event such as this can have remarkably positive repercussions. It may take just a split second to connect our "crazy" reaction to a certain life movement. Once we see it, we can bring it into the light. We can gather more overt data, but the long-obscured information that comes through the body, through dreams, through the multigenerational subpanel, can be reflected back to its original owners. "Oh, I see. I share this with you. I don't need to carry it all."

Certainly, none of our ancestors, close or far – the prisoner or the guard – will be brought back or brought peace through our suffering. If anything, our doing well is a balm for those who stand behind us, whether the slain of war or an alcoholic mother: they paid a price, and still, through us life goes on. Perhaps it will be in a good way. We cannot relieve them of the burden of their suffering, but we can relieve them of the burden of *ours*.

If we have received difficult messages from the past, we can send beautiful messages back. The message is in our joy, our fulfillment, our greater ease with the present, and with finding pleasure in creating greater continuity between what we reach for and the permission to actually take it into our hands and hold it as our own.

Our forbears' sacrifices gain greater meaning as we take life in and feel able and welcomed to contribute something more to it. Our contribution will, by definition, include something of them, our parents, grandparents, great-grandparents, ancestors as far back as time itself. In this way, with this expanding image, we can honor the past rather than join with it.

Brevities 10

The original sense of belonging tells us much about our later belonging. When it doesn't feel right or safe to extricate from the old portrait (as we first saw it), the same feelings of lack of safety or strangeness stick with us in everyday situations where belonging is the underlying issue – everything from work or marriage to our church group or book club. We seek places to belong, even if it is on the mountaintop with goats.

Sometimes we are clear that the narrow image from the past is of our parents or one parent. It seems impossible to take that image in any differently; the imprint is so clear and strong. And the truth is that some memories are truly difficult, even intolerable. The abusive parent, the critical parent, the addicted parent, the victim parent – still, life-force can be ours, even especially ours, for the taking. Connection with them in the already-established language of this part of the family is untenable. Perhaps you have already tried that, are attempting it now. Hating him or her or them for what was/is, you may have a hard time controlling your temper with your children – or maybe you are wildly permissive, afraid to exert influence. Or perhaps you would never allow yourself to have a drink even as you wonder sometimes if you smoke a little too much pot. Or maybe you are very strict with yourself, making sure that you never appear weak. Your friends describe you as distant, while you know that if you show vulnerability, they won't have any use for you.

These are the conundrums we find ourselves in when we seek to erase pain or circumvent it. We become absorbed in navigating perilous paradoxes: what we want at odds with what we feel is permitted. Sometimes a sense of over-entitlement compensates, but, of course, that gives up so much: integrity, self-respect, respect from others, balanced engagement with the world. Paradox.

But if we look for how the relationship between the person and the problem is tethered – where is the (k)not – we can begin to imagine how that relationship might be interrupted in a good way. Somewhere near the source of the problem is the resource that can help to initiate a new, refreshed sense of well-being. A glimpse of this larger image changes something, immediately loosens some tension, widens and softens our gaze. Suddenly, we are not only staring at the *problem*; right beside it, in the larger landscape, is the *resolution*. Maybe a breath is in order. Our compass has been slightly recalibrated.

Brevities 11

The thing about the family-of-origin is that it is what runs through us. DNA is shared: carrier of genetic information. DNA is shared: Dreams, Narratives, Associations. We are the consequence, and the next best chance. Wishing that our parents were different or that siblings could be different takes us away from life. The wish is passive and possessive, we wish it instead of changing ourselves; and it, in turn, grows bigger and bigger, taking hold of our energy, imagination, life-force. The wish puts us above and below, never at the level we need to be. Above, we think we know how things should be, how it would be better if. Below, we don't allow ourselves to come out from under the burdens that others carried; we simply take those burdens on as though they belong to us.

Expanding the image that provides our information is not about wishing; it is the opposite of a wish, it is a statement: I declare the right to imagine that things can be different. From there, you discover that things are. What came before is bigger than I knew. This is an implicit truth. From my position, I only know part of. There is, in addition to what I have settled on as my story – an extension of what I think is our family story – a parallel truth.

This idea of opening the landscape, allowing a wider lens, and getting out of the dyad is partly to permit this parallel truth to arise. The parallel truth is always the best part of the system wanting to support us, wanting us to go forward. Whether that best part is 86% or 2% doesn't matter because that's where we are going to turn our attention. In some therapies we might deconstruct the reasons that people did things to us, deconstructing those reasons within an understanding we generally already have, within a dyad – generally within the same language – and then we are left with the task, after some understanding, of either cutting ourselves off from the "toxic situation" or else embarking on the strange and never-ending road of forgiveness. Neither option invites a shift in where we stand in the family – they are strategies to deal with difficulties. One or the other may get us through this challenge, but then we may have to start out again when confronted with the next trigger.

Seeing the parallel truth, we can actually relate to a different part of our system, a different aspect of our parents – the part that by definition loves and supports us. That's a very different thing, not a strategy of proximity, a strategy to figure out proximity – that's a change in the self. And if you only change your strategy of proximity, that's all you change, and forevermore there will be triggers in the world that set something off because they resonate with something outside of conscious awareness that still exists. With the parallel truth, you move the point of resonance, not by changing anyone or anything, but by revealing another, greater point of resonance. We seem to be drawn to try to harmonize with the loudest beseeching in our family systems, the sound we heard first, but it is only the deep undercurrent of life-force that has the tone and tenor to harmonize back.

Thus another, more positive point of resonance or point of reference requires moving out of any dyad – dyad with the mother or father; dyad with a specific family member who suffered; dyad between the older and younger self. All foster a kind of tunnel vision where opportunities for positive resolution are suffocated.

In the case of the child-/adult-self dyad, once we begin to associate with the larger aspects of our original image, allowing fullness and fruition to be supported by it, we feel ourselves big enough to shelter the child self – something our mother or father or other was probably not able to do.

When we let the child lead, we become angry with the child, feel like failures, become self-critical and frustrated, because the child is not capable of meeting the needs of the adult. Maintaining our two parts in conflict ensures that no forward motion can be possible. Finding ways to allow the adult to become larger, by virtue of being connected to the larger context, that bigger self can begin to house the little one. The little self (the one who is back in time) can't do the job in the present world, not really. It is problematic that the child self is often the one who chooses the spouse, for example. She may choose the spouse on the basis of the feeling that she needs to be cared for, or because he is a bit absent himself and so won't demand too much. When the child is speaking more forcefully than the adult, running the show in a way, decisions are being based on a very edited version of the self, a distorted sense of one's capability and worth, and the other person is not being seen. Say the partner is an overbearing, short-tempered personality – the child self of the mate will likely do anything in order to uphold the contract, no matter how painful or demoralizing. At the same time, she'll have a sense that it is not right, or that it's not working, and so she will be angry, dissatisfied, disappointed, and probably blame him. The child self makes the decisions because simply getting older didn't change the inner picture of the unsupported child doing everything, shouldering everything to keep the world together.

Parallel truth. So, begin to imagine your parallel reality picture; for example, where Dad was dictatorial, controlling, all the bad words. When we open that picture a little, we see that Dad's father died when he was very young, and then we see that Dad's controlling nature is in his effort to negotiate the loss so that he will never feel lost again. This isn't so much about compassion or forgiveness, but about logic. It wasn't about us, and we don't have to live as though it was. It came to us, but it wasn't in judgment of us. The dyad loosens.

When we can see that he is actually turned in the direction of his own father, looking for his own father, asking where the hell he is — then the energy that comes toward us is softened. It is. We can actually hear him differently, even as he says the same words. We can feel the impact differently, and perhaps we can break the contract of merging or rejecting and feel some greater mobility. In loosening or widening the interpretation of the relationship, we dislodge the problem of it inside us. And if you can really *see* that he is turned toward his own father, you can actually keep him as a father and not lose him to anger (replicating his loss), keep him in your gaze but have more peripheral vision, begin to take in more of the system, including places where life is just beautiful, free, and full. And even with your father, the sentence becomes something like, "With all the pain that you suffered, you went on, and I benefited. Thank you." That's the grand manifestation of the part of him that was able to choose life. That's the part of him that you can connect with. And that's not a strategy – that's a stronger, more reliable heartbeat. It's the ultimate cardio exercise.

GATHER ENOUGH FIREFLIES

Brevities 12

Another consideration: a child loves both parents, even if one is absent. Every child loves both parents equally. That's upon birth, upon landing. It's way before we get to say, "Well, not really. I don't like Dad." It's upon landing. Things get divvied up pretty much immediately. If there's a split between our parents, we're going to find a way to love them both – where it is permitted and where it isn't. In other words, we're going to find a way to love them both that does not endanger our survival. Therefore, if Mom is present and Dad is not present, I will love Mom, be loyal to her, because she's right here and I need her. Keep in mind that this will also give me reasons to be angry with her down the line, because I am not free, but I will likely maintain a delicate balance between resentment and loyalty. Now I have to find a way to love Dad too. But in order to stay close to him I have to find a secret passageway. The hidden corridor often looks like: "I'm going to be like you" – angry, addicted, a failure, sick, whatever. Father will be represented. So love through loyalty and love through being like.

With regard to merging, the further we run, the more merged we are. Maybe we spend a whole life railing against the injustice of

Father, his bad habits, his shortcomings. We spend a whole life railing against him and swearing never to be like that or marry that. Who is the guide here, the North Star? Daddy. So we may have run across the world to get away from him and there he is: right in the mirror. This type of opposition is a powerful bond.

In cases of adoption or blended families, there is a temptation to forget the biological parents – both or one or the other – but because it is a "forgetting" and not a farewell, it tends to cause difficulties for their child or children. Why do we assume that a child cannot hold love for more? Why do we force him into choosing either/or? When the family, adoptive or in some way extended, can hold everyone, the child feels seen whole, accepted whole, agreed to whole. What a gift of caregiving that we do not replace or erase where the child actually comes from, but instead stand gently at the crossroads now, the thresholds now, the blind corners now, the moments of burgeoning possibility now. Is that not enough? Or is it just right? And could we extend that generosity to ourselves?

Once we see all this, we can begin to imagine ways to bring those feelings of loyalty, rejection, and identification to the surface and reconcile them in a better way.

In order to find a way to do things differently we bring the larger images to mind that we spoke of earlier. With our parents cared for from behind, by their parents and their ancestors, we are freed up to simply love them. While we may continue to be invited in by our parents to help them sort out their issues, we can stop volunteering for the job. We can stop defending her by being against him; and we can stop defending him by taking on his most challenging traits. No longer locked into a position of either collapsing with the strain or shutting down completely, mobility and creativity become our trustworthy guides.

PART ONE

Brevities 13

From an integrated place, where the backdrop is large enough and sturdy enough to support our bursting into a bright and colorful bloom, comes an ability to stay in tune with life unfolding. Staying up to date in our relationships – with partners, children, employers/employees, friends – is an essential part of staying in accord with the rhythm of life. The balance of give and take is the currency of present exchange. When an imbalance goes unchecked in a relationship, it chips away at the relationship in ways that are deeply unconscious and damaging. Not wanting to address an imbalance because we are afraid of losing her or hurting him may only be partly in present time. Remember the body exploration: where in my body do I feel it when I think of asking for more or giving less or demanding less or in some other way accounting for myself? What is it that I feel (not think)? How crazy is that? Where in the history might it not be crazy?

The balance of give and take is relatively simple to decipher if we are fully present. In present time, it's even okay to make a misstep. When a fear of expressing what we need or even expressing our love feels dangerous, perhaps it is. Perhaps we have made choices from a place not in present time, and so present-time desire is threatening.

Imagine: I love this job. My boss sees me as her confidante. I am special to her. I am not paid well, and I really do need medical benefits, but when I think about asking for a raise or benefits, my whole body begins to tremble. I cannot do it. Then she tells me about her date last night, how few people but me would understand, and suddenly I am flying high. Forget the raise. I'll take this home. Tomorrow I'll worry about the rent. I hate this job.

It makes no sense to anyone listening, and is probably infuriating to hear to over time. Somewhere, the whole thing makes sense though. Is it simple? Mom singled me out in the family as the confidante. I carried all of her secrets. I didn't want to know so much. It meant being against my father, but I couldn't bring myself to betray her, or ask her to stop, I couldn't lose her. Or maybe it is something further back. How many of our forebears suffered at the hands of others and were tortured, banished, or killed if they attempted to call attention to the situation? Either way, if I can disconnect the current circumstance from the early image, the trembling will calm (no longer in the body of the very young child), the fear of loss will be softened, and the current question can be weighed with greater clarity. What is really at risk? Is it really at risk? Is there life outside of this situation?

GATHER ENOUGH FIREFLIES

Brevities 14

The balance of give and take requires a little imbalance to stay in accord with the ebb and flow of life. Life is all ebb and flow. All inhale and exhale.

It's good to keep up, to stay in the present by finding ways to refresh and replenish, keeping up with love, with friendship, with all manner of relationships. We are careful not to be lazy about adding nutrients to the soil – those efforts come back to us in blossoms, in fruits, more life.

And we keep up with areas of deficit too. Where there is no reciprocity, we can update those areas too. If flowers are not blooming, something is out of balance. Perhaps we are over-watering or not giving enough attention. Perhaps there is not enough sun. Perhaps we are in the wrong relationship. If we stay in the wrong relationship, giving mightily to it but receiving nothing in return, we miss out on other possibilities – and they miss out on us.

We can begin thinking in this way – fully here and accounted for – when we allow the past to be completed and the present to be large.

Brevities 15

The only way to balance what our parents have done for us – giving us life – is to thrive. It's the only gift of any enduring value. The truth is that the only way that their contribution to the ongoingness of life is worthwhile is if life is ongoing. Our parents, in having us, declared faith in life's continuance – whether they did so with grace or grit. And that's our moment. That's the declaration out of which we come. That's the moment we build on. That's the moment that is ours.

Beginning to receive life in a less encumbered way, we announce to the world the best part of our parents. The image isn't of turning *back* to give, but of turning *forward* and making our full-out contribution. That's true with the ancestors too. That's the order of things. We don't attempt to push the boulder back up the mountain. Love flows down. And we make a decision: What is it we're going to do with that love?

Brevities 16

When the adult in us chooses a relationship, the partner becomes less important in the sense of "there's nothing else in the world but this person, I depend on him/her for my very life" but simultaneously more important in the sense that "with all the people in the world, all of the possible options in any given moment, I continue to stand beside this person." The first is a very young relationship that carries forward the parent-child relationship on some level: "You are everything." "I would die without you." "I can't survive without you." "Nothing else in the world but you." An extension of a parent-child relationship. But turning to the future together is something more like: "There's a lot in the world, there are a lot of people, and still each day, I choose you."

In early relationships, we are particularly in the thrall of system meets system, where the child who is missing a father is drawn to someone who is missing a mother, or one of five children may be drawn to someone who grew up as an only child. These are simple, common examples. And there is nothing wrong with these arrangements, of course. Love is love. In the first case, the couple may run into trouble eventually if, for example, reconciliation is made with the missing parent. If the man reconnects in a good way with his mother, perhaps he will shy away from the very maternal partner. When he has his mother, he may want a woman, a sexual partner. By the same token, a woman who rediscovers a healthy relationship with her dad may suddenly find her partner's protectiveness suffocating rather than attractive. The agreement then will need to be revisited. In fact, the original agreement has been broken, and some new clauses need to be added and old ones taken away.

Because everything is moving and everyone is moving, there are moments in a relationship when people are not in accord with one another. They may describe themselves as feeling distant or disconnected. But if one can say, "It's okay, I'll wait for you" or "I'm coming, I just need time," then that may be all the reparation that's required. "I love you. It's spacious. There's room for moments like this." Present time acknowledged, shared space noted, connection confirmed.

On the other hand, if one is clear in her heart, "I cannot wait," then it's important to note that too. To stay in a relationship unhappily is destructive to both parties. "I am staying with you because I am obligated to, but I see you as small, or I don't love you, or I have no respect for you." What a terrible message. Freedom holds possibility; ambivalence holds a chronic death rattle.

And if people can leave each other with love, then it can be complete and whole. The more the heart can hold the more trust is engendered. If the previous relationship, a previous important one, can be valued even in the farewell, the next relationship will have a good chance. When we drag along the tail of the old relationship into the new, we don't fully engage with the new because we don't really leave the old. It's a disservice to both people and to the relationship itself.

The person who doesn't complete the first relationship before entering the second one never fully lands in the second. The only way to complete is through gratitude. Often, people should have left the relationship earlier than they did (those overwhelming feelings from the past created confusion), and so completion is more challenging, gratitude is harder to discover. When we are unable to value the current evidence, to even see it sometimes, we are usually listening from another time and place. Everything is in whispers and fog. And often such violence has been done, emotional violence, that by the time we do wake up to the present it is very difficult to reclaim the love that brought us together in the first place. Rather than taking responsibility, we may wait for a tornado to actually hit before we gather our things and seek shelter. The emotional violence, then, serves a certain way of doing things: a child's way.

Brevities 17

Any bit of adult ground we can gain is a gift to our children. Any image behind us that we can allow to expand is a gift to our children. We can be easy portals for life-force – or we can make it so that it must come to them through a pinhole. No matter what, once we have given life, we have given everything. It is accomplished, on one level. "More" is a choice each day. As we lean back into the vast landscape of our own source, we can be comfortable and pleased with an expanding vision rising before us. If we are still steeped in our own dissatisfaction, and tethered to the deflated images of past disappointment, it is difficult to really allow, in the deepest most vital ways, our children to thrive (and fail and accomplish and fall down and get back up again).

If our children look to us with the sense that they have to do something for us, to be someone for us, their landscape of possibility is narrowed. Like us, perhaps, they step out of present time, and begin life somewhat out of sync with the now.

Still, they will likely flourish; life has a way of insisting. But we have the power, the brilliance, to make it a more easeful journey.

PART ONE

Brevities 18

It's important for couples that do not have children to find their meaning together. People often choose each other in this way: you and me against the world; you and me against our families; you and me against the past. At a certain point, though, the relationship moves from "me and you against …" to "you and me in …".

So, this has to be figured out. What does it look like when the couple gets to that moment? Something of meaning, something just ahead, draws the attention of the couple in a positive way. We can't look into one another's eyes forever. We'll run into walls. We ask too much of that person when we look to them for everything.

And if we think about why it is that we might be doing that, what might the answer be? Probably not much to do with the other person in a personal way. Who am I really looking at? Well, maybe my father. Someone who filled my view at a time when that was a matter of survival. Where is he? Or perhaps this gaze is in accord with an early sense that, for instance, I must stay vigilant because I am afraid Mother will

Part One

leave; I know in my bones that she is drawn elsewhere, perhaps to her own mother.

A young insecurity looks out, and perhaps asks too much of a partner. It's a good place to wonder. Where am I in time when I am with you? Orienting question. And then, what will we do together? So something of weight is helpful to a couple, to an individual, and to the world. A creative expression of love toward more.

Brevities 19

Of course, a child, or a meaningful shared project, does not magically keep a couple together. Again, being in present time helps people know what they know. When children are involved, especially young children, everything takes on greater charge. Imagine descendants several generations ahead. Imagine they are looking back to us. Did we complete what we needed to complete so they don't have to? Did we leave too much unaddressed, unanswered, so that the details may die with us while the fear (grief, anger, misery, sense of failure) is certain to be a legacy?

Part One

Brevities 20

"We will stay together for the children." In general, that's not staying together. We will stay here in this house, you and I, and we will whittle away at respect, kindness, and love. I will eventually destroy you (or let myself be destroyed). But the real thing, that's what the child knows. The children know what's beneath the Band-Aid, what is seething under the stitches. The charade is designed to protect the couple.

Alternatively: We will find a good distance, so we can continue to respect and to remember in a good way. To look at our child and see her father and say, "Wow. I love that about her. I love him in her." "I look at her and see the best of us, of him and of me." That's a good feeling for a child, to be loved with everything, Mother and Father coming through. Sometimes distance protects love.

When the parents really look at one another to deal with their stuff, the child is let out of the loop in a positive way, even if the parents are not getting along. What happens when mom is really, really mean to dad, really disparaging of dad? If she doesn't stand across from him and tell him, but rather tells the daughter that he's an idiot?

That child is not free, that child is stuck literally, physically in that entanglement and has to negotiate it. Often these are the kinds of secrets children are asked to keep. They're asked to hold stuff that belongs between the parents. If the parents simply turn toward one another, the children are set free from a dialogue that is not theirs to reconcile.

Part Two

Brevities 21

Mindfulness brings spaciousness brings peace. Mindfulness is about being with the present, whether that means truly listening to the person who is speaking to you or allowing a flash of anger to move through and then out or embracing the silence and calm of the moment just before dawn or getting out of the way of an oncoming car. It means a million things as it is defined by a million "nows."

When we are able to discern between the "was" and the "is" of our lives, to welcome the full breadth and dimension of all who inform our body, mind and spirit, we become more mobile and more confident. No longer entranced by the faulty images (faulty in that they were not complete) we absorbed as children, we can make decisions based on knowing what we want rather than avoiding what we don't. Confidence in the parallel truth – the antidote to those captivating images of terrified Mother, isolated Father, dead baby girl, grief-stricken survivors, massacred villagers, and whatever else – carries us on the wings of an entirely fresh understanding: we can honor all who went before by making the most of life now.

Honoring keeps us connected in a good way even as it lets us go into the celebration of our own way.

Mindfulness, then, can be supported and truly permitted as we embrace this level of reconciliation. Full attention to this moment is *the only way* to really demonstrate loyalty to everyone and everything who came before. Connection to them is not in question; how we do connection is a matter of infinitely creative choice.

Without updating the essential scaffolding of early knowledge, experience, and imagery, the practice of mindfulness can fall by the wayside with our other practices. Good

PART TWO

practice, like good advice, must resonate with our internal geography in order to take root. When we expand the geography, which took its initial shape long ago, we extend the spectrum of positive resonance. But as long as destructiveness, depletion, and misery make deep recent and historical sense, even wonderful options wilt in the soul.

Let mindfulness (or any other good practice) anchor and be anchored in a burgeoning consciousness of gratitude and abundance and it will have more natural harmony with your internal wisdom. Thus its "practice" will have an organic place in the mind, body, and spirit.

Brevities 22

In the present, everything is urgent and yet there are no deadlines. This simply means that we don't know how much time there is, so anything we want to do, we should always be moving toward. Simultaneously, the social pressures to do this by that age or to stop doing that by this age have little impact if we are in accord with the movement of life.

If we are in a job we hate, for example, the daily passive misery of it is a sticky waste of time. We need to look, immediately and clear-eyed. Is it helping us pay our rent, and are we actively seeking other opportunities along the way? In other words, are we grateful for what we have and then using the spark of that bit of abundance to galvanize our efforts toward something more?

The other way, the sticky way, is that we use our energy against the reality of the circumstance and satisfy our cravings with complaint and bitterness. This way of being begs the question, for whom are we waiting? Who do we think will change the situation? What long-lost disappointment, sense of atonement or guilt, do we have to reconcile before we can enter present time? Do we feel guilty about doing better than Father?

Are we caught in Mom's fear of change? Are we secretly atoning for some wrongdoing our family was a party to, or, alternatively, do we stand with the victims of some injustice, afraid to be seen? In what part of the family or community field does the vocabulary of self-defeat make sense?

PART TWO

Brevities 23

The narcissism of despair. Maybe the phrase strikes home. Despair is a position that has severe limitations. People who reject their family of origin navigate the world in a lonely way, an isolated way. They tend to ask too much of the world, even as they feel they ask nothing. We may feel the world owes us. Operating on the old barter system – I will not abandon you, for example – we expect recompense. Isn't it time the world make up for what we lost? But sacrificing ourselves is not actually a contribution to life. It is a way of stopping time, even as time itself moves on.

Isolation from the larger currents of life leads to continuing despair, a kind of righteous pain, and as the days and years and decades pass, layers of judgment, defense, regret are added until we literally can't see other people. The narcissism of despair can be such an overwhelming force that we literally don't understand what is happening in our interactions with others. We are overly sensitive and simultaneously have no compassion. Living in the specialness of our misery, the outer world seems foggy and untrustworthy, and the inner one feels empty.

Part Two

This is what is unique about us: the particular pain we experienced. We may have learned along the way to be satisfied with this idea that this is what makes us unique. Of course, we also know that it isn't true that our pain makes us worthy.

On the other hand, the contribution we make to the world can enfold "pain wisdom" in a good way, one that helps others. Rather than refer repeatedly to itself, our experience can be a bridge to compassion. From straw to gold. With everything we have – including what we don't – we make this contribution to the world, make meaning in this way. But in order to get there, we have to move from the very cozy misery of the past into the open range of the present.

Despair as a way of being has so little energy that others really don't notice a person who has adopted it. The past when dragged forward is a cocoon that protects us from the present, even from the joy that it may offer.

PART TWO

Brevities 24

Oddly, neediness is a type of self-sufficiency. Because it stems from an incomplete movement in the past, it lets other people know that there is nothing they can do to satisfy what is being asked. In general, they will just stay away. And when they don't, we push them away because we know that they cannot quench our hunger. Nothing will be enough. We are insatiable and self-sufficient.

When we step into that more expansive sense of how we are in the world and how the world is within us, we can become less "self-sufficient," less past-oriented. In accord with life means in accord with its natural flow, its movement. Stepping into the sweet unknown, we are in shared space. We share that we do not know what will come next, what surprises await. We are separated in what we do know, in what has happened already, and will happen again as we recreate or replay it.

One. I am walking with a friend down a beautiful path that neither of us has ever been on before. As we look ahead, and side to side, enchanted by the colors and shapes and gentle smells, maybe even a tiny bit nervous about where the next curve will lead, she and I feel giddy and close, glad to have company, easy and present and full.

Two. I am walking with a friend down a beautiful path that neither of us has ever been on before. As we look ahead, and side to side, I am remembering walking down another path with my mother. She is depressed again, being mean to my sister. All I can think about now is how awful that felt. Suddenly, I am crying and I stumble on a rock. Goddamn it, I scream, it was right in the middle of the road! My friend looks confused and disappointed. Why didn't you step over it? I look around at the trees and the flowers and her hair glistening and at my feet (not a child's). I realize I have no idea where I am, or who I am with.

Three. I am walking with a friend down a beautiful path that neither of us has ever been on before. As we look ahead, and side to side, I tell her about the image with my mother. She looks at me and says that she too has some difficult memories. We look at each other, really look; we know something about each other's pain, are both human in that way. We agree in that moment: let's notice the breeze and the colors and spring perfumes. Let's pay attention right here and now.

PART TWO

Brevities 25

Maybe every problem indicates an interrupted movement: where we got stopped (in our mind, in our understanding, in our sensory knowledge, in our being able to know more) because we were afraid of hurting somebody, because we were afraid for our lives, because we were making up for a sibling who died before us, a parent's loss of his or her own parent at a young age. Lost in time, we didn't get to find the right way to navigate for ourselves, not really knowing where we ended and others began. So we keep trying to find the right way to do that, to complete the movement, and each time we do, every situation, every relationship, contains those old things, and also contains new complications.

One has the option of surrendering to the futility of such endeavors. Hm. This may be the first good step. Fighting it, trying to beat it, may very well keep us engaged, too busy to wonder if there isn't another way, or a hundred. Relaxing the tension between our problems and ourselves is perhaps the first thing we have ever done differently. The problem may still be there, but we don't have to stand directly across from it – we can move to the side and look from a different angle. A sidelong glance is good enough.

By submitting to our powerlessness to change what is beyond us we may then have the energy (the life-force, time, and right) to admit our true power: being able to shift internally and orient more toward what we desire. In this way, we begin to move from discontinuity to continuity between past and present, what was and what is. Dichotomies change into sequences, always moving towards more … more peace, more meaning, more love.

Brevities 26

In close relationships, whether with life partners or friends, it is interesting to imagine this sentence: I agree to you exactly as you are. You can close your eyes and just let it roll around your mind. I agree to you exactly as you are.

Agree, not accept. Agreement is active, equal. Acceptance is placing oneself above or below, as in resignation. Agree.

Now what if we cannot say it, cannot imagine feeling it? Then what is it that we are really feeling? Just the other side of sentence, right? I do not agree to you as you are. Interesting.

Important for the other person to know, important for you to know. I want you to be different than you are. I want you to be someone else. Wow. Present time.

Brevities 27

I agree to myself exactly as I am.

This is even more interesting. Again, agreeing, versus accepting. This is not a statement of resignation. It shouldn't be.

It is a new beginning. Present time.

Part Two

Brevities 28

When we are strongly against something or someone, we add to the tension (and sometimes violence) of dichotomy. Instead we might wonder, what can we do next? Opposition is an easy place to slide into. Sometimes it feels like power. Ultimately, though, it doesn't really satisfy, it doesn't come from or contribute to a sense of personal dignity.

When a situation is close by, sometimes it's hard to pause before reacting. But reaction is immediate, shortsighted, shallow-breathed. Response, alternatively, allows for creativity. Again, the bigger landscape helps us pause, and pausing allows us to breathe, and breathing lets us find the dignity of wholeness.

In interrupting the impulse to react, even to direct challenges, we are expanding the landscape for ourselves and for those who come after – our children and grandchildren, and even beyond. Creativity is nuanced, powerful, generous, generative, strong. It is the way to meet every obstacle and to welcome every opportunity – creatively.

Part Two

Brevities 29

Access to creativity – not limited to creative expression as in painting, dance, music, or writing – and its lack have implications across all dimensions. For example, when we feel that people avoid us in social or professional situations, it may be that we exude a kind of need or deficit without being aware of it. Others may keep their distance not so much from us personally, as from an energy that puts them on alert. They may not be able to articulate the "it," but they know to feel some fear or anxiety that tells them to protect themselves. It is a prey instinct, in which they feel that the energy of want is going to vacuum them up somehow.

Those who do respond to this energy may themselves need too much — to be attracted to a wounded bird in order to feel big. This scenario ultimately destroys freedom. Freedom to what? To grow.

So, there is creativity in the sense that each day, each moment, is a fresh chance to gather in our sense of self and imagine the unique ways in which we might contribute to the ongoingness of life. This is not so different from bringing familiar words together in an unfamiliar way and creating a poem that touches someone, or many. What comes back from this single creative gesture cannot be known before the gesture is made. The poet shows him- or herself to the world through the creative expression of pain, love, joy, observation … and the world responds. Some move toward.

In life, we have access to creativity in everyday ways: a kindness without expectation toward another, a pause to notice the fireflies, taking a different path home, rising a half hour earlier in the morning to write a letter to the day, a sweet memory remembered and a gentle promise made to take our next steps in honor of that time. Creativity helps us stretch our muscles, widen our heart, fill up on life. Then, when we connect with others, perhaps our energy is different, not appearing to need too much, but instead having something to offer.

Part Two

Brevities 30

We carry both the scars and the gifts of the past. Imagine that a captivating being crosses your path and asks who you are. Which will you show her first? Which will you show him first?

Imagine that that being is life.

Brevities 31

"Life will take care of me" is a very different statement about myself than "I will take care of life." One looks more for signs and serendipity, where the other looks for opportunities to contribute.

PART TWO

Brevities 32

If a gift is given with an expectation of return, it isn't a gift. If the exchange is aboveboard, then everyone has the opportunity to participate (or not) because it isn't a gift, it's a contract. If the expectation of exchange is covert, then it is a manipulation. This is true when I give my husband a present while secretly hoping for something in return or when I give a homeless person a dollar and get angry when she buys a beer.

In good exchange, what I *take* from giving can remain private – it makes me feel good (not better: private, not comparative); I am so grateful for what I have (that gratitude has overflowed into giving, private and respectful); over the long road, we embrace a balance: I hold out my hand when you are tired, as you have done for me (the reciprocity between us is private, no need to call attention to itself).

Life is filled with subtle exchanges. It is helpful to gauge our place in such dialogues so that resentment doesn't pool internally and disrespect get released inadvertently.

Part Two

Brevities 33

As life wears on and the time for dreams is diminished, reality can take on the sheen of normal possibility or the gray pallor of disappointment. It is a choice whether or not to keep in step with time, to respect its passing and to cherish its gifts simultaneously.

Brevities 34

If I see myself only in the mirror that you are holding, I am always susceptible to the inherent distortion of another's judgment. This is so whether that judgment diminishes me or elevates me, whether it is negative or positive. Instead, I have come to understand the importance of trying to see myself first before I look at the reflection.

Brevities 35

Making plans is good. They can keep inviting you along, even when your mood shifts to a darker place. They can keep you focused and at ease, even when the surrounding environment is in flux. How we create plans is important. They must be clear enough, serious enough to hold us as we hold them. At the same time plans must have fluidity. This is a word that houses resilience, flexibility, attunement, creativity, growth. Like the river that bends when the ground curves irresistibly, that leaves things behind when necessary, that picks up and carries new things downstream, even though sometimes dregs, that pushes through even when it appears to be choked by obstacles through no fault of its own, and that eventually joins with a body of force much bigger than itself – complete and still changing. Like ourselves too, complete and still changing.

Part Two

Brevities 36

You might ask how I can possibly expect people to be optimistic in the face of the most difficult events in the course of a life. First, I only expect it of myself, and even so, it's more a request or reminder. Second, I have come to experience optimism not as a fanciful perspective predicated on naiveté or denial but rather as the only truly practical way to navigate the world.

In the past, I did think of cynicism as being realistic and optimism as naive. Now I see optimism as clearly being realistic, in absolute accord with reality. The truth is, dawn has not once let us down.

Optimism keeps us open to creativity; creativity keeps us in good contact with optimism.

Part Two

Brevities 37

When we make amends to another, it must be in tune with the other. Otherwise, it is simply a continuance of the offense for which we are apologizing. An imposition of our will. In other words, making amends must not ask anything of the other, not even acceptance. It is a unilateral act that restores balance. And we always know what it is.

Brevities 38

We know ourselves through the stories we tell about ourselves, and we know the world through the stories we tell about it. Others know themselves in this same way, and know the world in the same way. When the details of these stories clash, the illusory Tower of Babel falls. Where we thought that everyone, at least in our "group," spoke the same language, perceived the same images, now it seems we are on our own. "This is how I know myself" is undermined by "This is how I know you." And vice versa.

Part Two

Noam Chomsky is asked about his first memory and he says it's of being required to eat some oatmeal. He refuses and simply holds it in his cheek. He locates the memory at about 16 months. He marks this (lightly) as perhaps the beginning of his lifetime of "whys?" Why must one do this? Why does it work this way? Does it? So, is this his earliest memory because it is a good beginning to the story he tells himself? Or is it already an image in the longer story of his family, cascading down through generations? Does it begin at 16 months, conception, or before our parents even begin to tell the story of us as a part of their story?

Brevities 39

All belief systems have as a part of their foundation the repudiation of other systems, primarily based on the assumption of superiority of one set of beliefs over the other. It is the implicit dismantling of other that leads to disagreement, even violence, as systems rub against one another. In politics, we know this leads to paralysis. In personal relationship, it leads to the same thing. Our belief system – an amalgamation of threads from upbringing (including rejection of upbringing) and influences from our environment – anchors us amidst the chaos of everything outside of us (and inside of us sometimes too). The cluster of our beliefs serves as our protection against becoming unmoored in a sea of wild unpredictability, and so a threat to the system is a de facto threat to our security, to our safety and sanity. Whether we chant, pray, sing praises, or rail against belief systems, we must necessarily find some cover in the face of an untethered life. Perhaps that's the common ground, a recognition that we are simply trying to find our way. Perhaps then we don't need to impose our solutions on others as a way of feeling secure.

My way is better for me.

GATHER ENOUGH FIREFLIES

That is perhaps the most difficult period to place – to let it be the end of the sentence, to indicate the end of the thought, to not go on to say that it is also better for you. In fact, that period may be the most important punctuation mark in any relationship.

Part Two

Brevities 40

The ultimate chaos, of course, is death; it usually surprises us even as we nervously try to prepare for it from birth. Death is moody and unpredictable, and when it arrives, it will not tell us where it is taking us. Life ultimately always runs into it but when, where, and what exactly, are mysterious. The stakes are high when we are talking about the time we know – five days, or ten, forty-seven, sixty-three, ninety-eight years – and they are even higher when we are talking about the time we don't know. He lived for this length of time … How long will he be dead? Thus, belief systems, whether it's simply lights out, no more; ascending to heaven or descending into hell; returning to life as another being; well, our belief systems can be especially tender when it comes to the subject of death. We seek to protect ourselves and those we love from the uncertainty of eternity.

Each day is a gift. This is how I know life, and thus its absence too.

Part Two

Brevities 41

So much of our stress and tension comes from holding on to what *was* in the now of what is. Recently a friend told me that she was frightened because she'd heard that her medical treatment would cause fatigue. As I spoke with her, I realized that the fear was rooted in a distorted idea that things should remain the same even as change happens. My suggestion was to accept fatigue, make friends with it even. Listen to a great audiobook rather than fall prey to disappointment, despair, and anger about not being "on the go" as usual. As life changes, we constantly need to make adjustments to the mechanisms that get us the nutrients we need; otherwise, we face starvation every time the wind shifts.

Part Two

Brevities 42

It's been observed by innumerable people and expressed in countless ways, still I am always struck by our impulse to try to change the world rather than ourselves. As impossible as we know it is to change the world, we must suspect that it is even harder to change ourselves!

GATHER ENOUGH FIREFLIES

Brevities 43

A mom told me that she wanted her daughter to be able to spread her wings, to achieve all that she was capable of achieving. Then she added that she didn't want her daughter to be like her. What a terrible sentence, a sentiment that can annihilate the dream for both. As this mother denigrates herself to herself, she does the same within her child, denigrates her essential aspects as they flow through her daughter. After all, her daughter is of her. I remember when I was very young my mother always saying that she was ugly and that I was beautiful. When I saw myself in the mirror, I saw quite plainly that I looked just like her; then I knew she was lying when she said I was beautiful.

GATHER ENOUGH FIREFLIES

Brevities 44

A young woman whose father had died recently was upset because she hadn't found a way to thank him for being her father. As in most families, there had been strife, and she had grown distant. But she had also more recently begun to reclaim her gratitude to him, to soften her negative judgment of him – and consequently of him inside her. In this movement, her communication was already accomplished. And as she speaks of him later, perhaps to her own children or nieces and nephews or friends or to her self, his story will be one of greatness, completeness, humanity. Gratitude engenders a richer legacy for all.

Part Two

Brevities 45

We grieve for what we have lost. Sometimes we grieve for the time that has past. Sometimes that grief for time contains as many tears as when it is about the loss of a beloved person. Beloved time that when we had it we took for granted. Beloved time that we wish we had taken more seriously, treated with greater respect. Beloved time that we measured in minutes and hours, trying to rush ahead of it or hang back behind it. Beloved time that even now as we mourn its passing, we lose.

Brevities 46

The child in the photograph who looks back at you, what does he or she need from the adult who holds the photo in hand? The child is locked in time – afraid, proud, confused, ecstatic, lonely, dazed, innocent, still. Let the child know that you have a place in your heart for him or her, a place from which to watch as life goes on in a good way, a place where the image is no longer frozen in time but warmed by possibility.

Each day is the day to begin again. Whether things are going well or are challenging, we recommit to the present, taking neither pleasure nor pain for granted, but allowing for expansiveness no matter. To share the pleasure – expanded. To keep reaching out for guidance on how to work with the pain, and to receive each piece, even the tiniest, engaged, thankful, willing – expanded. To complete each day so that we may rest at night, and then with the new light – bright or overcast – to begin again.

The child in the photograph who looks back at you, what does he or she need from the adult who holds the photo in hand? Only this: a place in your heart as you move beyond the stillness.

Brevities 47

Taking responsibility is a concise action, whereas taking on blame that doesn't belong is never-ending. When I take responsibility for my part in an interaction, it is full, confident, refreshing, neither beseeching nor expectant. Taking responsibility leads to freedom, including from the other and his or her fate, whether the narrative of my decision is to leave the relationship or to rededicate my heart.

PART TWO

Brevities 48

When one is betrayed, the loss of ground is usually difficult to recover. Betrayal's opposite is loyalty, or trust. If I am loyal to you, I am in accord with the trust you have in me no matter the push and pull of people or events. This is a strong and delicate intimacy. Thus when it is forfeited to something else it is felt deeply and for a long time. Your trust in me is a gift you give me and betrayal is a way of discarding that gift.

When we speak of betraying ourselves, the same holds. We give the gift of trust to ourselves and in betrayal we cast aside that gift in favor of something else. What could be more important than trust? The need to sidestep fear.

The greatest test of trust is fear. Even at the heart of greed there is fear. Fear of not having enough. Fear of not being able to achieve what we want within our own integrity. Every time I betray you, I betray myself first. Trust has no latitude, no "sort of," no ambiguity. I know it always. Am I trustworthy to myself, to you? I always know the answer even as I wonder. Already I am slipping. The question might be more accurately written: Am I afraid? Afraid of what? Afraid of anything, afraid enough to toss the gift of trust by the wayside when that allegiance reveals my position before something or someone who might disagree. Once the gift of trust is released, I no longer have a position: I do not stand by you and I do not stand with me. I am a traitor. Now I am no longer afraid. I am a ghost.

GATHER ENOUGH FIREFLIES

Brevities 49

When I am in disagreement with someone, I have learned to check in with myself rather than immediately judge that person. Then, perhaps my idea shifts. But even if I stay with my idea, this initial movement allows for opposition to flow into something bigger that can hold us both. Where once I might have hardened into a process of "against," I am curious.

Brevities 50

After a lifetime of criticizing my mother and my father, how good it felt to finally agree to them as they were – and as they are within me. I hadn't realized how exhausting it was to harbor the secret fantasy that I might change the past until I acknowledged that secret and put it to rest. How refreshing now to know that actually, something much more is possible, as shifts continue to take root in the open space of gratitude.

Brevities 51

At some point, if we are lucky, we meet others who by virtue of their love or their enlightenment or their pain or their compassion or simply their willingness to accompany us for a while reveal to us ideas that are not in our original canon of thinking. When we are introduced to these ideas, rather than allowing the threat of difference to overwhelm our ability to receive and understand, perhaps we are able to pause, to soak in the light of another; and with weapons and shields laid aside we may sit with unfamiliar thinking, swish it around in our head without judgment, and let it have its time and place for minutes or moments or more. If we cannot hear or will not listen, our thinking will remain pure – pure even of the beautiful, though sometimes messy, prospect of growth.

GATHER ENOUGH FIREFLIES

Brevities 52

Certain topics should rarely if ever be discussed. I can feel even as I write this that there are things that seem to immediately divide. Some topics fall squarely in the realm of belief even if we pretend that they don't. If you *need* to convince me of the rightness of your *belief* or I *need* to persuade you to mine, perhaps it is related to something more than what we are calling "the topic."

Discussions are fields in which we may back and forth in an easy or rigorous way. We may listen and learn from each other, be passionate, and able to back down, then

Part Two

laugh and return to love at the end of our discussion.

Beliefs are fields in which our ideas tend to be rigidified, seemingly informed by some greater force, perhaps serving to protect our family in a previous time or our tribe or village. These convictions cannot move, they are steeped in the deeper realms – of war and poverty, threat and sacrifice, terror and loss – but we cannot identify these contexts in the moments that our triumph-or-else-be-defeated convictions rise up.

Discussions lead to more; beliefs tend to lead back to themselves, and cannot be freely shared; rather, they insist on being asserted.

PART TWO

Brevities 53

How difficult it is when anger is our closest companion, judgment our protector, withdrawal our oasis. How different is the light when we step off this certain path. How different when we whisper farewell to anger, judgment, withdrawal. It is lonely for just a moment, and then other companions begin to arrive – openness, ease, engagement. Soon, what is deliberate becomes natural, a new path, delightfully less certain.

Brevities 54

When we look to the future, how much do we depend on the particular vision we have? The more strenuously we hold to its details, the more likely we are to lose its essence. If we feel that we must hold fast to a specific image, fight for it above all others, we might suspect that the future we look forward to is actually stuck in the past – either an attempt to bring back something we miss or an effort to create its opposite in order to escape what was. Thus, as we take steps toward that envisioning, we soon find we are actually circling back, back to a place we never really left behind.

PART TWO

Brevities 55

Whether we know the best doctor or the most potent secret remedy, pray to the right deity, understand the deepest philosophy, or are privy to special guidance from the cosmos, thinking we can save another has some very big presumptions under its cloak.

First, we assume we know what salvation means in the given situation. Already we are out of connection with the person whose experience it is. Almost immediately our efforts become obstacles in their path. And, undoubtedly, our wanting to save someone has more to do with us than them. We cannot bear his pain or we couldn't save one of our parents or we are seeking justice or revenge or meaning. Now aren't I dragging that other person into *my* fate? Don't others become pawns in my psychic landscape, and perhaps lose their footing in their own?

But what if we instead imagine simply accompanying others, walking alongside them on the road as they walk alongside us, all of our resources easily accessible should they be requested? Possibilities burst wide open because we are all looking ahead. Never losing sight of our own destinations, whether close or far, we free our companions from our own needs – even our need for them to get better however we define it.

Part Two

Brevities 56

When you hear the laughter of children in the playground or watch couples strolling down the street hand-in-hand, and it makes you angry, what is at work in your heart? Bitterness has very little juice for anything fresh in life, anything different from the sour taste of past disappointments. The dry and withering do not fare well as the future unfolds, they soon get caught in the wind and disappear in the far gone.

If, taking another path, you allow the sounds of those children to pass through your senses like a beautiful melody or waves breaking at the shore, and imagine the strolling couples as moving like sails in the breeze or colorful birds in the tree, you may awaken to find that you still have a place in the lively parts of life.

Part Two

Brevities 57

In the darkest night of the heart, gather enough fireflies and recall the light.

GATHER ENOUGH FIREFLIES

A Little Background

This book is greatly informed by the teachings of *Bert Hellinger*. His body of work, commonly known under the heading of Family Constellations, is a synthesis of wisdom gleaned from the worlds of philosophy, psychology, art, and the magnificent interiors of the thousands of people who have come to him for guidance. What makes his teaching so powerful, in part, is that it does not separate threads of understanding: Lao Tzu joins Aristotle, who is walking alongside Freud, who is in deep conversation with Rilke, as the rich textures of Wagner's musical phrases waft through the trees, and the streams of Ericksonian therapy, gestalt therapy, transactional analysis, 20 years in the Catholic priesthood, engagement with Zulu traditions, training in group dynamics, and early life with Mother and Father all flow through the landscape.

178 I do not speak for Bert Hellinger, and this book is not about him or meant to be a literal translation of what he teaches. It is most certainly inspired by him. What I am able to give back to this truly brilliant teacher is to pass on what I have learned. Suddenly, this is a pleasure, though this book simply scratches the surface.

Family Constellations is the popular phrase used to describe Bert Hellinger's work; however, as the work evolves, he has used other phrases, including Movements of the Soul and Spiritual Family Constellation Work. At the heart of the work are always Hellinger's profound insights about love, order, and conscience, which continue to grow as he and his wife Sophie continue to explore an ever-broader terrain. A major aspect of the work that captivates one's imagination is that in the workshop setting, there is an emphasis not only on the insights but also on the participants' resonant representation of a family system, and much beyond, to witness and embody revelations on myriad levels.

GATHER ENOUGH FIREFLIES

A Guide to the Entries

PART ONE

1 – recollecting family – 3

2 – the problem as guide and connection – 14

3 – change is a process – 21

4 – fixing the past – 22

5 – dependence and first commitments – 26

6 – broader image of dyads and generations – 29

7 – replication, trance, and life-force – 35

8 – accord with life's momentum – 41

9 – the everyday weight of past events – 48

10 – belonging in the past and present – 58

11 – discovering the parallel truth – 62

12 – overt and covert love for both parents – 73

13 – the balance of give and take – 78

14 – updating relationships – 83

15 – contribution balances the gift of life – 85

16 – choosing, renewing, and leaving partners – 87

17 – a parent's gift to the future – 94

18 – a couple's meaning for the world – 96

19 – tying up loose ends – 99

20 – staying together for the children – 100

PART TWO

21 – anchoring mindfulness and discernment – 105

22 – grateful or bitter – 109

23 – the narcissism of despair; its solution – 112

24 – in the shared space of the unknown – 116

25 – completing interrupted movements – 120

26 – agreement to others – 123

GATHER ENOUGH FIREFLIES

27 – agreement to self – 125

28 – opposition and creativity – 126

29 – creativity in daily living – 128

30 – scars and gifts – 132

31 – taking care – 133

32 – giving freely – 134

33 – impermanence – 136

34 – looking in mirrors – 137

35 – changing plans – 138

36 – optimism – 140

37 – amends in tune with the other – 142

38 – stories of self – 143

39 – systems of belief – 145

40 – in the face of death – 148

41 – in the face of change – 150

42 – the hardest thing to change – 152

GUIDE

43 – diminished selves – 153

44 – a lost parent – 155

45 – lost time – 156

46 – the child in the photograph – 157

47 – responsibility – 159

48 – trust and betrayal – 160

49 – curiosity before judgment – 163

50 – agreeing to the past – 164

51 – listening to teachers – 165

52 – discussion and conviction – 167

53 – the new companions – 170

54 – looking to the future – 171

55 – accompanying and saving – 172

56 – in the face of life – 174

57 – gather enough fireflies – 176

GATHER ENOUGH FIREFLIES

Acknowledgments

With deep gratitude to you …

Evelyn Tucker, my mother; Edwin Friedman, my father; Edwin Friedman, my older brother

Julius Stauber, Pauline Stauber, Patricia Tucker, Carrie Tucker, Louie Elie, Peter More

Bart Walton, Cole Tucker-Walton

Suzanne King, Elizabeth Hershon

Diana Canova, Tamar Rogoff, Hollis Barickman

Jeffrey K. Zeig, Bert Hellinger, Mark Wolynn, Anne Linden Steele

Rhonda Schladand, Tim Schladand, Joyce Crum, Steve Schumacher, Claire Khudai Dagenais, Rosalba Stocco, Tatyana Britton, Karen Passalacqua, Arlene Nelson, Michelle Blechner, Judith Crop, Lauri Shainsky

Omega Institute, especially Susie Arnett and Brett Bevell

Cristina Casanova, Jan Crawford, David Friedman, Joanna Crespo, Samuel Morett, Beth Hand, Karen Terceira – and all of my students who are equally my teachers

Made in United States
North Haven, CT
06 August 2022